THE ART AND LITERATURE OF THE MIDDLE AGES

ART HISTORY LESSONS

Children's Arts, Music & Photography Books

Speedy Publishing LLC
40 E. Main St. #1156
Newark, DE 19711
www.speedypublishing.com

In this book, we're going to talk about art and literature in the Middle Ages. So, let's get right to it!

Art in the Middle Ages varied from region to region in Europe. It also varied depending on the span of time. Despite these variances, the styles of art were distinctive enough that they can be divided into three major periods: Byzantine, Romanesque, and Gothic.

IC
XC

EGO SVM LVX MVDI
S BARTOLOMEVS
MARIA
S IOANNES

The majority of paintings and sculptures during this time period were based on somber religious themes. They were displayed in Catholic Churches so that people would be able to see religious scenes while they were worshipping at mass. In addition to paintings and sculpture, artists of the Middle Ages were masterful at metal work and engraving. Beautiful stained glass windows were created for cathedrals and manuscripts were written and illustrated by hand. Mosaics made from small tiles were sometimes created instead of paintings.

WHAT IS BYZANTINE ART?

The beginning of the Middle Ages is also referred to as the Dark Ages. This period lasted from 500 AD to 1000 AD. Most of the art produced during this time period was art in the Byzantine style. It was produced by artists living in Byzantium, which was the Eastern Roman Empire.

Coronation of the Virgin
(St.Maria in Trastevere, Rome)

LEVA EIVS SVB CAPITE MEO ET DEXTERA ILLIVS AMPLEXABITVR ME
VENI ELECTA MEA ET PONAM IN TE THRONVM MEVM

What were the Characteristics of Byzantine Art?

Prior to this era, art forms tried to depict a realistic look both in drawings of people and objects. Byzantine art was instead concerned with symbolism, especially in regard to religion. The figures in Byzantine art look like icons instead of real people. The backgrounds were frequently painted with gold colors so that the spiritual figures seemed to be suspended in mid-air.

Coronation of the Virgin (St. Maria in Trastevere, Rome)

ΜΡ ΘΥ

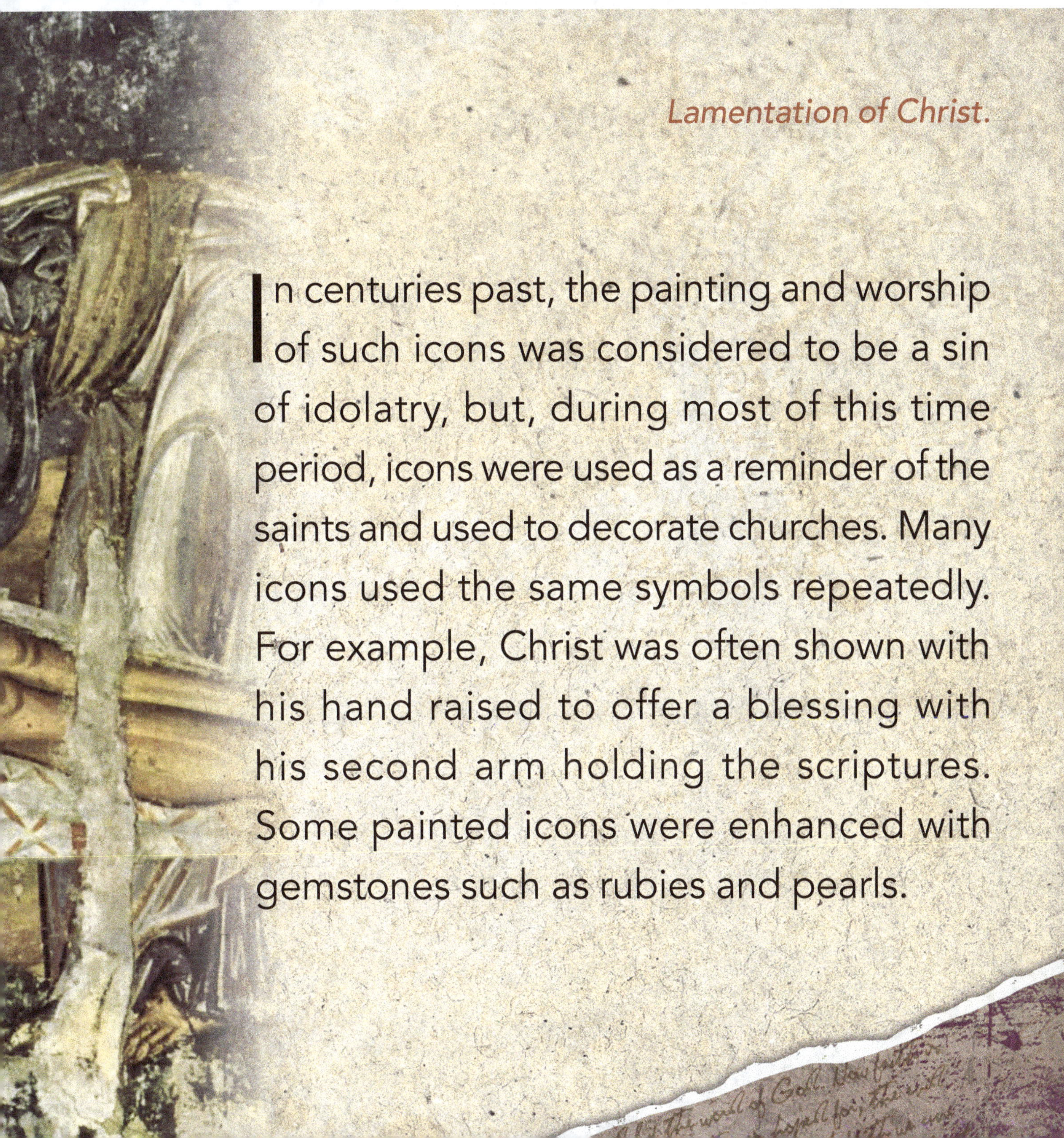

In centuries past, the painting and worship of such icons was considered to be a sin of idolatry, but, during most of this time period, icons were used as a reminder of the saints and used to decorate churches. Many icons used the same symbols repeatedly. For example, Christ was often shown with his hand raised to offer a blessing with his second arm holding the scriptures. Some painted icons were enhanced with gemstones such as rubies and pearls.

Religious texts, such as scriptures from the Bible as well as manuscripts that were used as devotionals, were illuminated by hand, which means that designs were added by artists along with the handwritten text.

There were two periods of time between 500 AD and 1000 AD when the use of icons was banished. This was between 726 and 787 AD and a second time between 814 and 842 AD. These periods of time when the work was banned are called iconoclasms. The word ***"iconoclasm"*** means ***"breaker of icons."***

Ὁ ΑΓ
ΓΕΩΡ
ΓΕ Ω
ΓΙΟC

WHAT IS ROMANESQUE ART?

The Romanesque style of art began about 1000 AD and lasted for about one hundred and fifty years until the period of Gothic Art started. Sometimes art directly prior to this period is labeled ***"Pre-Romanesque."*** As its name implies, Romanesque art was influenced by Roman art. However, that influence was blended thoroughly with Byzantine Art as well.

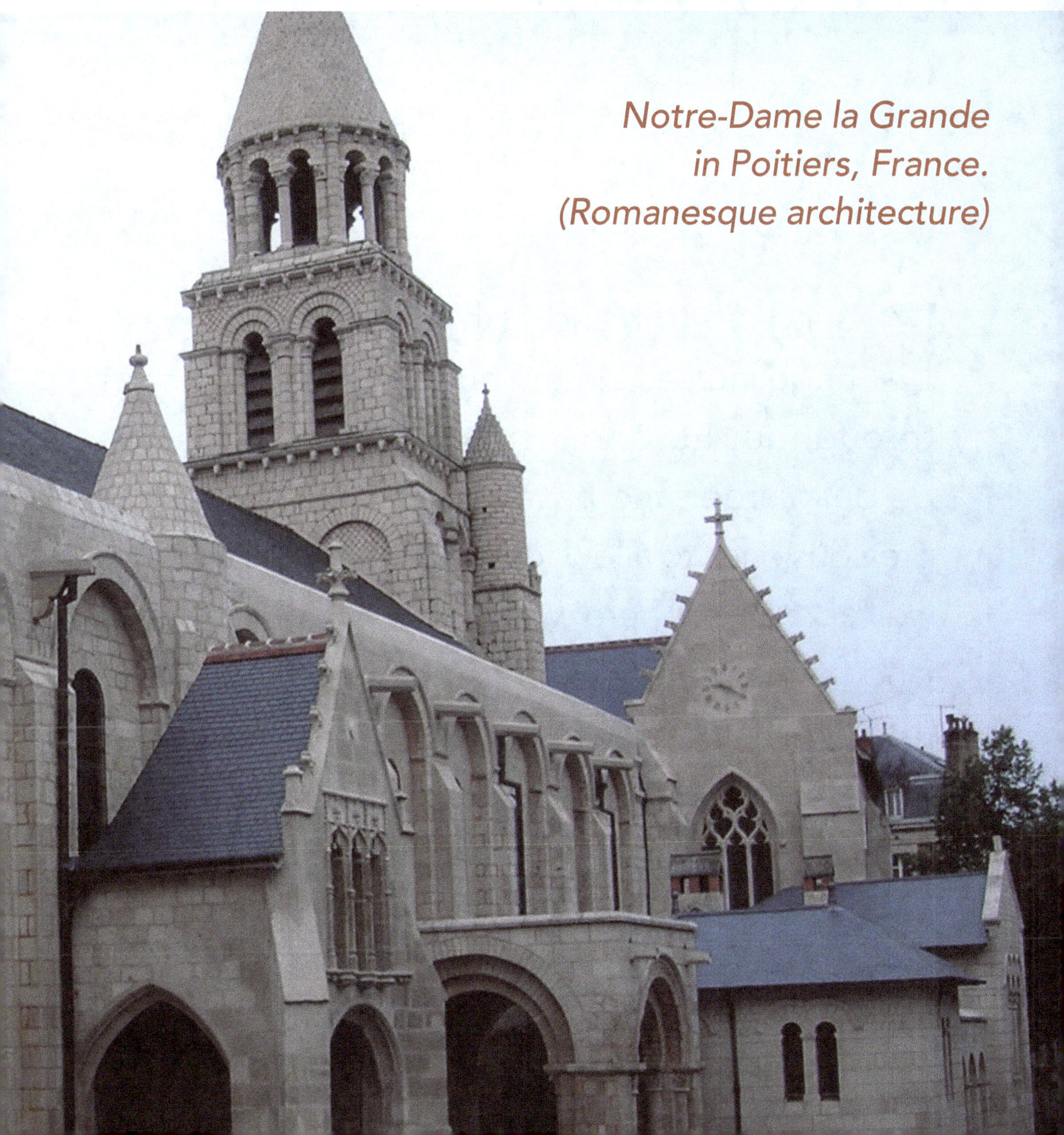

Notre-Dame la Grande
in Poitiers, France.
(Romanesque architecture)

During the 10th and 11th centuries there was a huge increase in the number of monasteries throughout Europe. The churches needed to be built larger and have more decorations than previous ones to allow for the increase in priests as well as monks. There were also more parishioners who flocked to the churches to view the relics of the saints. As a result, the architecture of churches used the Roman arch extensively in their designs to allow for this more expansive space.

The focus of Romanesque art was still about religious themes. Church architecture included domed ceilings and detailed stained glass art. Artists carved the columns of the buildings and there were large frescoes painted on the walls.

WHAT IS GOTHIC ART?

Gothic Art began around 1150 AD and ended at the beginning of the Renaissance period. Artists during this period began to expand their styles to include much brighter colors and techniques of perspective that added a dimensional appearance to their paintings.

·S· nicolaus·
·S· bernardus·

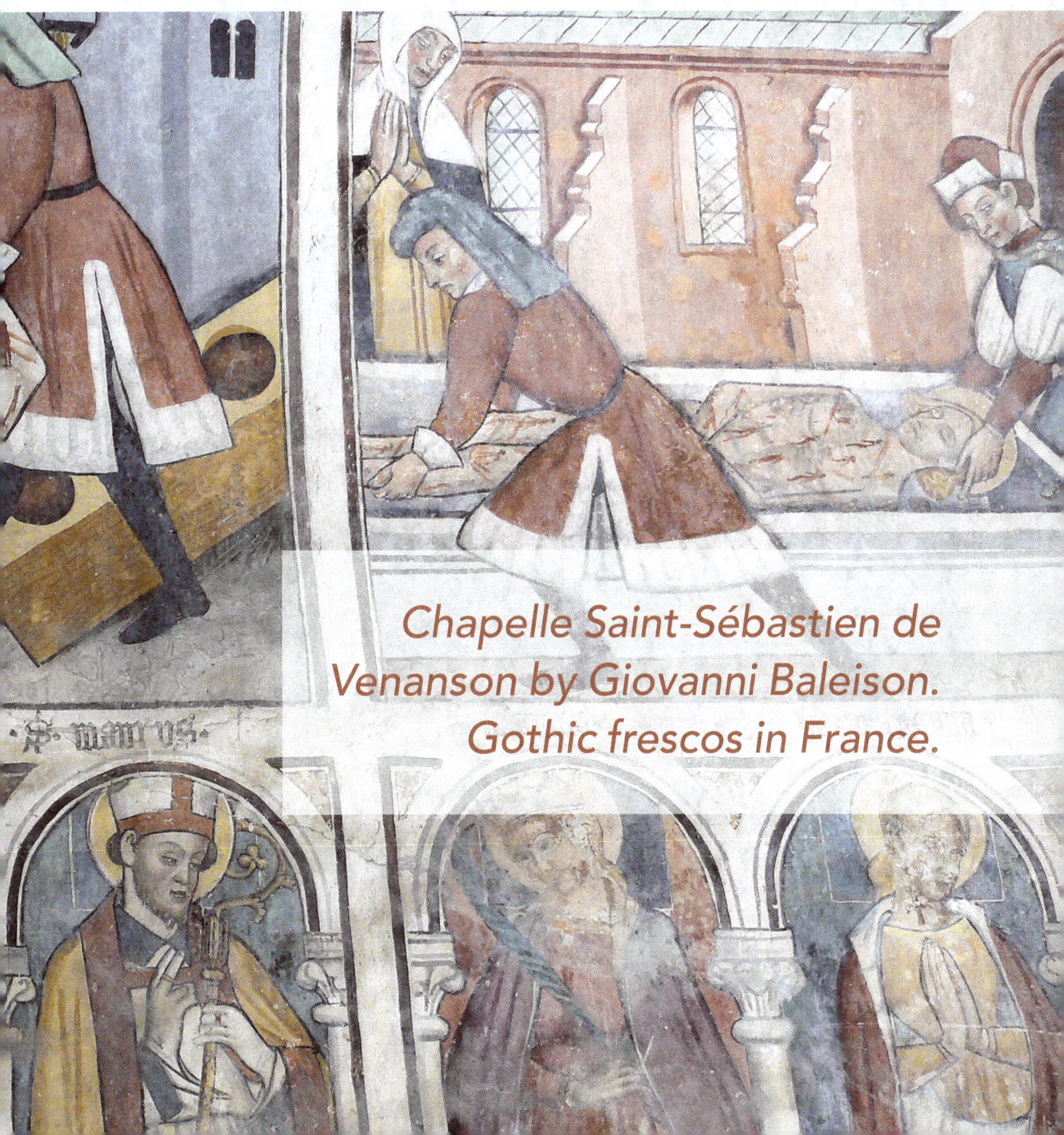

Chapelle Saint-Sébastien de Venanson by Giovanni Baleison. Gothic frescos in France.

They worked with shadows and light more and got away from the flat appearance that was typical of Byzantine and Romanesque art. They also started to move toward more realism in their work. The subject matter of art expanded to include animals in mythological scenes as well as the traditional religious subjects.

LITERATURE IN MEDIEVAL TIMES

Medieval Book

Most early literature during the Middle Ages was written in the Latin language. Educated people used Latin for both speaking and writing and in those days many of those who were educated were monks and scholars. The general population of citizens didn't know how to read or write.

Consideratio autem de Deo tripartita
Primo namque considerabimus ea quae
ad essentiam divinam pertinent; se-
cundo, ea quae pertinent ad distinc-
tionem personarum; tertio, ea quae
pertinent ad processum creaturarum
ab ipso.

Art and literature came together in the illuminated manuscripts during this time period. The *"golden age"* of illuminated manuscripts began around 1150 and lasted until Gutenberg's printing press was invented and printers had started to mass produce books around 1450 AD.

The reason the books were called ***"illuminated"*** was because gold or silver leaf was sometimes added to the intricate designs drawn on the pages. At the beginning, most of this work was done by monks for religious texts only, but eventually handmade books about different subjects were sold to wealthy citizens. This change encouraged new businesses that were run by professional scribes and artists who were not part of the clergy.

Most of them did not sign their work. This changed in the late Middle Ages because instead of being looked upon merely as craftsmen, illuminators were considered true artists. This change in status meant they sometimes signed their works or drew a small self-portrait somewhere within their manuscripts.

Important Medieval Texts

Because it took so much labor to create them, textbooks were hard to come by. One famous book of that era is the Ars Minor. This book, written in Latin, was copied by hand thousands of times and was used for monastery scholars who were teaching Latin grammar to their students. Other important texts were used to study logic, philosophy, and the origins of words, which is a study called etymology.

the word of God
hoped for; the

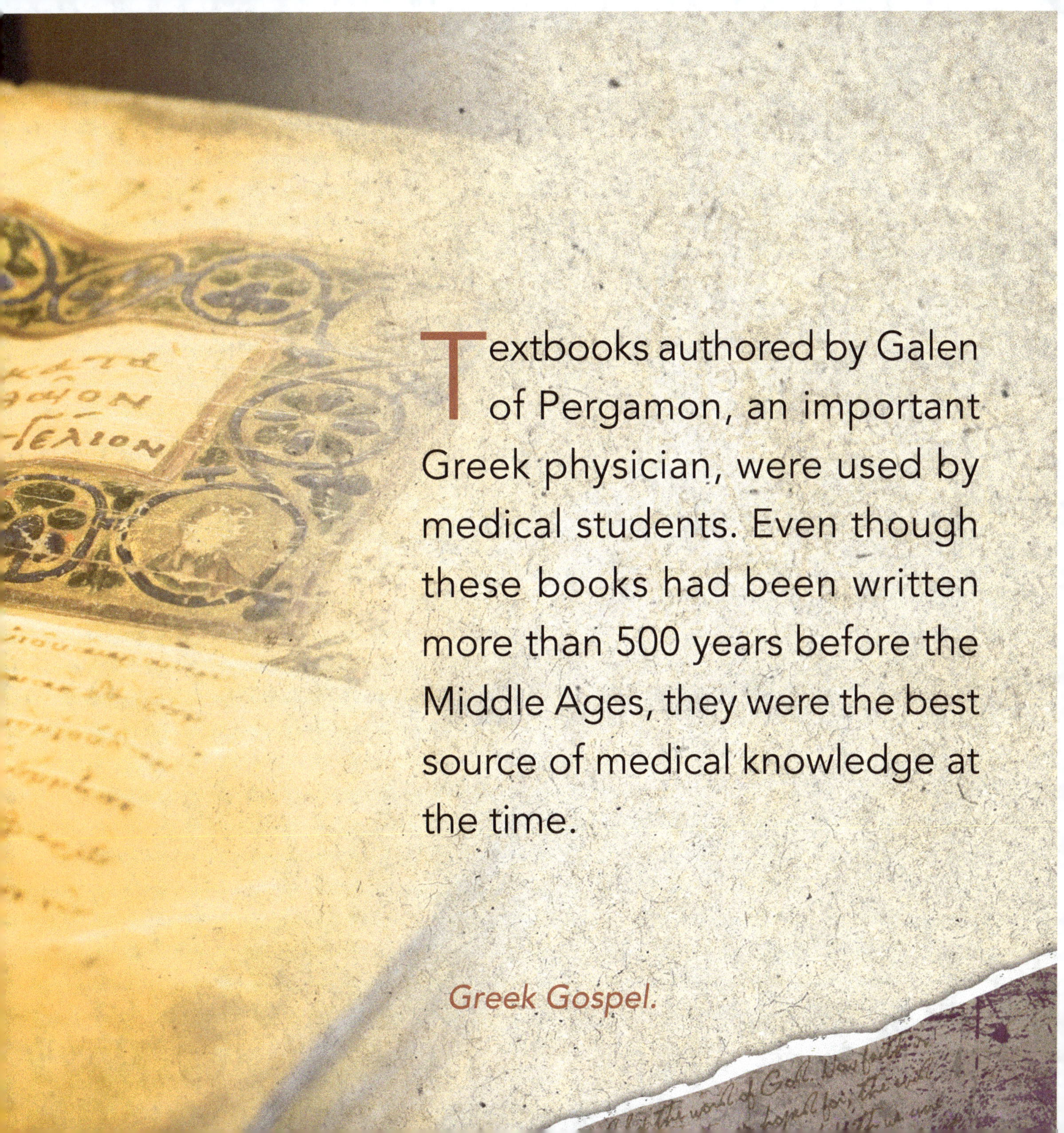

Textbooks authored by Galen of Pergamon, an important Greek physician, were used by medical students. Even though these books had been written more than 500 years before the Middle Ages, they were the best source of medical knowledge at the time.

Greek Gospel.

MEDIEVAL STORIES AND TALES

Many villages still had oral storytelling at this time. Stories were repeated thousands of times and passed from village to village. If someone took the time to write them down, they were more likely to be written in the language of the common people of that era. That language could have been Old English, Middle English, or French.

One of the stories that was written down was the story of **Beowulf**. It's written in Old English and is an epic poem written in 3182 lines of alliteration in which the Scandinavian warrior Beowulf is the hero. Throughout the story, Beowulf kills three monsters including a dragon. Only one copy of the poem still exists today and dates from 1010 AD. It was never signed by the author.

Two other famous stories told and written during Medieval times were **The Song of Roland** and **Tristan and Isolde.** The Song of Roland is written as epic poetry and tells the story of the Battle of Roncevaux, which took place during Charlemagne's reign in 778 AD. Nine different manuscripts of the poem survive today and they are all slightly different from each other. The story of Tristan and Isolde is a love story about a knight and a princess, which has elements that are similar to the much-later story of King Arthur's Camelot.

Er lieb herz sant Lon
ginus wz ein ritter zu den zeytē da
die Juden Jesum verzyetē.vñ mar
terten.vnd wz dabey da vnser herz am creutz
hieng.vnd nam ein sper vñ stach vnsern hertzē
in sein heylige seyten.Da floß wasser vnd blut
auß d wundē.Nun het d ritter blöde augen.
Da ran dz blut an dem sper ab dz es kam auff
sein hand.vñ vnwissent.Da streych er es vber
sein augen.Da wurden sy im lauter vñ klar.vñ
gesah gar wol.vnd der got der im sein genad
außwendig thet der erleuchtet im auch seyn
hertz inwendig mit seiner genad.vñ im ward
sein hertz erweycht von dē zeychen die da ge
schahē da Cristus gemartert ward.vñ gewan
groß rew vber sein sund.vñ bekant dz Jesus
d war gottes sun wz.vñ ließ sein ritterschafft
vñ hielt sich mit grosser demüt zu den zwelff
poten dy taufften in vñ lertē in den weg zu dē
hymelreych.Darnach ward er ein münich inn
Cesarea vñ het vnsern herzē gar lieb.vñ die
net im mit vleyß tag vnnd nacht mit vil guter
vbūg.vñ wz wol achtvndzweyntzig iar ein se
liger münich.vñ prediget vñ leret dz volck.vñ
bekeret manigē mēschē zu got.des ward des
landes herz innen d wz ein heydē.vñ gelaubt
an dy abgötter.vñ wz Longinus thet od sagt
dz het er fur einē schympff.vñ ließ in vahē.vñ
da er fur in kam da sprach er zorniglich.Lon
gine du solt deinē gelauben lassen den du die
leut lerest.wañ er ist gar ein spot.vñ ker dich
zu den göttern vñ bet sie an.des wolt er nicht
tun vñ wz steet an cristo.dz tet dē furstē zorn
vñ hieß im sein zuīgē außschneydē dz leyd er
gar gedultiglich vñ begeret in seinē hertzē dz
got mit im were.Darnach schlugē sie in iñ sey
nē mund biß im die ezen außuielē.dz leydē tet
im gar wee.Da halff im got dz er dennoch ge
reden mocht.Da ward er gar fro vnd dancket
got seiner genaden.

¶Nach dē nam d lieb heylig ein axt vñ zer
brach dy abgötter vñ sprach offēlich.last sehē
ob es götter sein.Seind sy gewaltig götter so
schat in mein gewalt nit.vñ da er dy abgötter
zerbrach.Da furē dy bösen geyst iñ dē furstē
vñ auch sunst in manigē menschē.vñ peynig
ten sy iemerlichē.vñ da sy in dē leydē warē da
vielen sy fur sant Longinū vñ batē in dz er in
hulff dz sy gesunt wurdē.Da fragt longinus
dy teufel end sprach.warūm seyt ir iñ den bil
den.Da sprachen sy da sein dy abgötter vnser.
Aber wo man Cristū nennet vñ ein creutz ma
chet da beleybē wir nicht.Darnach verloß d
furst sein gesiht.Da verstund sant Longinus
wol dz got den furstē habē wolt.vñ sprach zu
im.Du wirst nit gesehent noch von dem teufel
erlöst biß dz ich getödt wird.Da schlug mā im
sein haubt ab.Da fur sein sel zu dē ewigē freu
den.Da viel d furst auff die erden fur den hey
ligē leychnā vñ bat iñ dz er im vñ got erwurb
das er wolgesehent vñ erledigt wurd.das er
warb im sant Longinus.Da empfieng er den
tauff.vñ starb darnach seliglichē.Nun helff
vns got vnd sein gebenedeyte muter das wir
kummen zu dem ewigen leben Amen.

¶Von sant Gerdraut

Fables were also very popular during Medieval times. These short tales usually had a moral lesson about which behaviors were good and which were bad.

Another popular book was called **The Golden Legend.** This book, written by Archbishop Voragine told stories about the lives of saints. One of the stories in the book is the story of St. George and the Dragon.

The story that was most widely-read in the Middle Ages was **The Canterbury Tales** by Geoffrey Chaucer. Chaucer wrote the Tales in Middle English, which can only be read by a few select scholars today. Middle English was vastly different than the English language we speak today. Words were spelled very differently and when they were spoken, they sounded nothing like our English of today.

Heere bigynneth Chaucers tale of Melib...

The **Canterbury Tales** are filled with interesting characters from this period of time and each of them has his or her own story. There are descriptions of 27 different characters from all different walks of life in the story.

Canterbury Tales mural by Ezra Winter.

They are all traveling to the same shrine. The host of the group decides that they will each tell two stories, two on the way to the shrine and two on the way back.

Then, the host, whose name is Harry Bailey, will pick the best storyteller and that person will win a fine meal at Bailey's tavern. The stories vary from comedies to tragedies and provide a great deal of insight into different societies and social standing in England at that time.

Awesome! Now you know more about the art and literature of the Middle Ages. You can find more Art, Music & Photography books from Baby Professor by searching the website of your favorite book retailer.

Two medieval antique books

Visit

BABY PROFESSOR
EDUCATION KIDS

www.BabyProfessorBooks.com
to download Free Baby Professor eBooks
and view our catalog of new and exciting
Children's Books

www.ingramcontent.com/pod-product-compliance
Lightning Source LLC
Chambersburg PA
CBHW082057130726
48003CB00009BA/2883